ROSEBUD

Rosebud

A POETRY COLLECTION

Nick Jameson

INFINITE OF ONE PUBLISHING

For Michelle

Who will never have the opportunity to read me, and of whom
I was deprived the opportunity of getting to know better.

When your light went out, the light by which
we read was made a little less bright.

Even as love crowns you so shall he crucify you.

Even as he is for your growth so is he for your pruning.

Even as he ascends to your height and caresses
your tenderest branches that quiver in the sun,
so shall he descend to your roots and
shake them in their clinging to the earth.

From *The Prophet,* by Khalil Gibran

You'll arrive at your destination when you stop trying to reach it.

INTRODUCTION:
THE SEAFARER'S FOLLY

Directing himself towards his destination unknown leagues over the looming horizon, the seafarer falls in love with the stars. In the darkness of night they descend, as if a celestial blanket dropped from Heaven. Their lustrous light surrounds, comforts and calls him towards the unknown future. They form patterns that he traces with his mind, evoking myriad images to which he grants symbolic meaning drawn to suit his dreams.

His voyage long, his vision jumps from one bright promise to the next. He's certain one is the North Star, set to guide him to the promised land of everlasting love. But the star fades and, with time, crosses over the zenith and falls behind him. For long did it lead him, and never shall he forget the faith it fostered, but it's not *his* star, only an image of hope.

They come and go, these great blinking beauties of the night, illuminating and guiding him, saving him from being lost at sea. He swears that the brightest stars were made for him, and with each he becomes entranced. Enrapt by them, he believes one after the other to be the guardian of his destiny. Like heavenly hypnotizers, he's easily bound by their spells.

Every one of them passes over his nighttime skies, submerging itself in horizons lost endless leagues behind him. None shall he forget, and none shall be the one, each guiding and illuminating his path and granting him hope when it's needed the most, then quietly falling away. Yet never may he learn, for in the obfuscation of the sun-starved night he *needs* them, especially as his beleaguered craft is being mercilessly struck by storms.

So, holding fast, he points his craft at the horizon, open to every spell.

Torn to Shreds

Of the deep disquiet am I enslaved
Of passions turned and twisted
Of frail and fickle sensations
Of dire distress promising peace
Of an endless litany of loves unknown
Of faces bestowing rescinded bounty
Of beauty as burdensome as mass
Of bright flashing eyes subsumed by shadow
Of honors hoped in discarded heaps
Of battles cried yet endlessly unheard
Of every means of concealing the crisis
Of casks of wine and clouds of smoke
Of a life drifting away before being lived
Wrapped around a heart ever ready for battle

Left unshielded, torn to shreds

Petrified Tree

When the sacred-most seed fell upon my soil
        I barely noticed
My land was barren, neglected
Aching from a waste of space

When the seed sprouted
        the land took to life
All was fertilized by its growth

As the taproot descended deep within
        vitality spread across the grounds

Easily the root dropped to the deepest depths
Discreetly, quietly binding itself to the land
clinging to every particle of earth
wrapping itself around every rock

And up rose the most magnificent of trees

And the land praised it
        knowing it as everything it needed
        as everything the land promised itself

Birds sung of its hope and providence
As its blossoms bore the brightest fruit
        that never ripened
staying hard, high and out of reach
mocking the hungry below
        un-plucked, unbitten
forbidden, yet continuing to grow

refusing to fall to the earth

Too late, for the roots of this tree are engulfing
spreading so wide, descending so deep
        that they devour the land
        becoming inseparable from it
rebuffing all attempted extrication

And there it remains
        pridefully petrified

Entirely enmeshed with the earth
Never to be burned
Its fruit never to be eaten

It *is* the land
        the land belongs to it

Any subsequent seed to fall
can never deliver its roots deep enough
nor cast its leaves high enough
to ever generate new fruit here

So the land starves

The birds sing of empty stomachs
        of abandoned nests

The land forever longs for the tree to fall
        as they cling to one another with equal force

Honored Guest

Swimming in my breast with thunderous silence
Perfectly self-assured and imperishable
Refusing to follow ruling or precedence
Marriage and childbirth be damned

Hounding happily, then tearing at the tenderest flesh
Salvation and damnation lustily in league
Bubbling over, then sinking all the way down

Just memories, memories...

But remembered more by heart than mind
So to be perfectly preserved, as if by magic spell
Try to breach them with reason, I dare you!
To retreat from this sanctum, singed

It's as the subtle rhythms of pumping life
Of chambers that once welcomed the anointer
Endless hide and seek with the sanctum's servants
Lost to be found, only phantoms and echoes
Past pains and elations, forever renewed

Where are you, great honored guest?!
The only one that freely explored the sanctum
Enlivening, illuminating now frail and darkened flesh
Haunting the halls by which we know we're alive

Oxygen

I'll forever hold a flame for you

Forever

For this flame be the same as every flame borne by every breast
Fanned by the same oxygenated inspirations blowing life into life
Life in its totality, delivered across the expanses of existence
Whether self-importantly stamped as 'civilized' or not
Tending to burn brighter when not, as uncorralled wild fire
Not trapped by machine, production or profit, but burning for *itself*

Perfectly impartial, flames singing and
surging up from intrinsic eternity
Heating our halls, setting itself
upon dream and dread alike
Firing every order's exhortations,
carried upon torches towards every hope

It is *this* flame that I carry for you, that which warms all things
Forever burning and brightening, billowing and bursting forth
Everything once dark, filled with the glow of your long stolen flame

Time cannot extinguish it, as it burned before time
It shall burn into eternity, through every resetting of the clocks
Through every wisp of it passed into every hosting heart
At the very moment of divine manifestation of new life
At the very moment when the Holy Ghost parts the curtain
Dropping the robes of apparition, born into flesh once more

This same flame, *one flame*, carried since before it could be felt
Before it could be folded into the bellows of vitalized being
It is *this* flame that I carry for you, can you not see?!
My forever dream, flickering in red and blue ephemera
Endlessly recast reminiscence, the divided rapture of two

Be my oxygen once more, when once I took full breaths!

Revelation

The only time that I really know you
Is when we're wrapped around one another
When our expressions lose all lying
When our minds may no longer maintain their gulf

It's the gulf we all lay between one another
Out of fear, out of uncertainty, out of self-interest
Nothing said is entirely trusted, everything defended
Like fencing: thrust and parry, thrust and parry

Ever angling for advantage, veering for one-sided victory
Setting up fake targets to pull away at the last moment
Striking from hiding, where you should have known I was
Only learning when stabbed all the way through

Only lovers making love lose their guile
Only when they, when *we*, really let go
Only when mind and speech drift into oblivion
And all that remains is the body merging with heart

That refuge where we're reaching, interlacing tendrils
That's where I know you!
The you of no past, no future
No plans, no money, nothing to conserve or aspire to

A complete fidelity to the moment *only*
Let us find that truth again, and remain there!
Shhhh… no more talking, don't even think
Your intellect, your ambitions, they betray you!

Only heart and body
Only here and now
There's your truth!
There's your divine revelation!

Sentry

A preying mantis guards my doorway
Performing its rhythmic, beguiling dance
Stealthily shifting in strewn sunrays
Catching the mortally curious in its trance

Offering its projected pair of scythes
The death-dealing reaper is close at hand
Appearing a blowing flower in the breeze
Death dealt by naturally-ordered demand

Unnervingly darting triangular head
Twitching, springing, clutching claws
Waiting with perfect patience in the passage
To cut down the corpses upon which it gnaws

Yet this specific guardian is oh so special
Don't be caught by mere visual representation
For its arrival shielded me from temptation
Blocking self-destruction in my salvation

For this day I shan't go out
Being privy to her predations keeps me inside
My lustful longings have met their match
Behind this spiritual sentry shall I hide

Chatterley's Moon

Lady Chatterley
Oh so true
Lady Chatterley
Hail unto you

Magnificent minds make smallness of life
All that's felt, animalistic rot
But being alive is the edge of the knife
The thrill of a spirit that can't be caught

Self only known when throwing itself in
Nakedly sensitive to all that it's presented
Slipping by unheeded, untouched the sin
For every half-life is bound to be resented

So much time in my mind, wrapped up in it all
Philosophy, poetry, diving down in the deep
Intellect roaring, deaf to Venus' call
Bounding out from every yearning in which I steep

Unpeel your packaging, step into the fire
No heat, no passion, afraid of the flames
Running from risk, you're dousing desire
The temperate, careful life steadily tames

Listen yee intellects, yee speakers for God!
Self-righteously ascending to an imagined height
Through the muck of the ego you unwittingly plod
The moon wains while you shrink from the lustrous night

Sight Unseen

Oh so bounteous beauty
Beheld with every breath
Sickness in not seeing you
The unfelt inviting death

Poured forth forever freely
Peace that can't be bought
Ever the way of wonder
By the purest seers sought

True freedom knows one way
To want nothing but the now
To the magic in every moment
Does the divine within us bow

Salvation of the Sea

When did your toes last touch the
coarse, cool, salted sand?
When you took off your shoes and socks,
declaring your right to immerse?

When did you last smell the salty air, that
sweetly funky, enlivening stench?
Were you subsumed by the stress-silencing,
caressing sound of crashing waves?
Were you enshrouded by the coolly-kissing
fog sucked in from the savage sea?
Did you stand in silence, awing at the immensity
of it all, the eons of the untamed?
Did you behold the ethereal, scarlet-orange
sunset bounding off the shimmering sea?

Your feet sunk in the sand while there, *only* there,
not feeling like it was a waste of time?
Did you walk in the wavefront, legs numbing
and reviving, numbing and reviving?

Did you play witness to the seabirds competing
for fare, protesting enemy maneuvers?
Did you feel the seaweed grab and wrap itself
around your ankles, then slink off again?
Did you connect with the force of creation, the
cradle of life, reaching out for the Ancient East?

When was the last time?

Do you even recall?

No wonder you're unwell!

The modern contagion: *nature deprivation.*

Please brethren, like me, seek the salvation of the sea!

God Sometimes Plays the Devil

It's not depression.

Depression implies a listless incapacity to summon joy and passion.

It's more akin to *brutal unhappiness*.

Like being tethered to a ravenous beast that bites and claws,
leaving me alone to lick my wounds, only feeling the force
resurge when the beast's belly bulges.

For when the beast is sated, the passion is reignited,
the potential of purpose, romance and adventure
reengages my heart, beseeching my mind.

Then the beast turns back towards me, and my
heart is hacked, my mind is masticated, my fears
of the future are used to flay me, my longing for
lost life lashing out until I'm knocked to my knees.

How to untie the tether? Cut the cord? Afford myself
the possibility of lasting peace? *Only love.*

Love like an apple I've only ephemerally held,
and once brought to my face, but that's always
been slapped from my hand before I can bite.

It's as if God, wearing the red robes of the Devil, has decreed:

The fruit is forbidden to you, you who's been made

to endure this evil, for to actually savor the fruit
demonically-dangled before you wherever you go
is to satisfy and soften, and thereby lose thy
deprivation-driven will to join forces with the fullest future.

A More Comfortable Cage

In her youth, the lesson but a whisper, the trapping
responsibilities unknown, she looks to him for his
natural attractions, and his facilitation of fun.

In her twenties, the lesson being hammered
from every angle, the trapping responsibilities
looming, she looks to him for his
confidence, the latent capacity to make money.

By her thirties, the lesson long hammered home,
the trapping responsibilities leading her to her cage,
suckling pups surrounding, she looks to him for
the money that he's making.

By her forties, the lesson embedded and rusting,
life's iron bars set, pups being weaned towards
their own entrapment, she looks to him for
the money that he already has.

But how much can we blame her?

For this is the 'real' that the lionized parasites have produced;
the overfed leeches that we honor with the rotten word 'success.'

The real of master and servant, pimps and whores
euphemistically cited, enslavement by monetary means,
extorted with the purchasability of survival, comfort,
even freedom, and the ability to buy the ears of

politicians in this place of democratic pretense.

For there is but one lesson, and she's learned it, for you cannot
be so dense as *not* to learn the lesson when, again, there's but ONE:

Money or misery.

(Dedicated to the endless litany of greater loves lost in the
loathsome competition to craft a more comfortable cage.)

True Gospel

We are alive, gifted existence
Of eternal energy into matter are we manifested
Of the everlasting life of God, the energy
of all things, are we composed
The indestructibly everlasting One
made into the infinitely mortal many

Why are we here? What is the point?
Existence. The gift of the experience of being
For there can be no other purpose for
splitting the One into the Infinite
You've been bequeathed a part
of God, centered in your heart
It is your eternal flame to carry into
the gift of every presented moment

I say again, *the point of life is life itself*
For life to seek to thrive, not just survive
To make the most of the gift of every present
For every life carrying the eternal torch

Thus, the purpose of all things is to serve the God carried by us all
The essential of all things, the heart of spacetime and matter
Made into endless finite forms facing material decomposition
Decomposing down into that which cannot further decompose

And here, too, see the purpose of all resource
To serve the point of life, aiding in
the quality of its experience

When hoarded unused, amassed
unapplied, perpetrate a sin against God
For its limitless manifestations are
left unserved, its purpose dishonored

This is God, and morality, the heart of it all
This is the True Gospel, the reason for being
To feed the flame which we *all* carry
Fulfilled by the *only* spiritual sacrament: LOVE

To serve Life
To serve God

Unlearn the separation
For there is none

Schrodinger's Fate

Fluxes of foiling, fortunate fate
Cast up from warring eternity

Bludgeoned in back and forth battle
Of realization carried forth unrealized

Freedom of will forming in the cataclysm
Of this forever manifesting contest

Be one of failure or success?
The colliding truths of coexistence

The bestowing of armoring, weaponizing will
May be laid upon both sides of unresolved outcome

Heart hearing and heeding, guiding and pleading
Set in sensing, naked anticipation upon the sidelines

Who be you who knows what to do?!
Yet another idle interpreter, perchance?

You who are the vanquished
You who are the champion
You who are the interceder of fate

All of it is in your hands
Doubtingly falling through your fingers
As you conceive of your tragedy
Your will designing its defeat

Will you not take up arms once again?!
You who bears blade and shield of firing furnace!

Lit of the eternal flame forever within, never without
Granting the only means to strike for the future

Feel not the desperation of the faltering furnace
Cold with diffidence, fearing tomorrow's descent

Simultaneously seen from high above the battle
Impervious with hard won, static self-assurance

How hath your furnace become, my friend?!
Hungrily fed the fuel, or starving for flame?!

The Advocate Wears Red

Bibulous I may well be
But blue in the face, I assure you, I'm *not*
Tearing me from my endlessly taxing troubles
That sound of the glass filling with sighted faculty
In vino veritas, dripping in its ageless parlance:

This bottle is bottomless, as the well of your ink
Staining impassioned page, evoking the rise of undeath

Joyfully it revives the eternally-entombed mysteries
Indolently permitting knowing to creep past nerve
Making mincemeat of today's and tomorrow's torments
Filling the air with its fantastically-auspicious portent
Stealing fear, denouncing the delusions of despair
Burying the wanton of my worry beneath my will
Setting flame to the burnable brought before its bonfire
Leaving the lingering, unburnable ancients left to loiter

Bared before me, Spirit's beseech bounding from breast
Bridging with the Oneness with whom I commune
Clearing responsibility's remnants, the maggots of mind
Remaking modes of money and matter into dreamy ideals
Hurling provocations at nay-sayers and betrayers of beauty
Whispering of the wonders revealed in the aimless wander
Rebuking those affecting the holding of holy sacrament
Hearing what must be said, its patience outlasting noise

Won't you join me here, in this land of half-conscious wakefulness?!

Nay, you're being ground by the grind, for by the bard, it's but noon!

I opened the bottle because I wasn't supposed to
Little is so inspiriting as casting convention and expectation aside!

Hah! The wickedly-wily, instigating imp is at it again!

The Sharpest Knife

It cuts through almost everything, stopping in but
the one thing, revealing the apparently impenetrably
solid to be soft, and spread away at will:

The judgments and expectations of others
That the personal is unprofessional at work
The existence of preexisting, conflicting relations
The looming wedding, the plans for family
The age difference, surpassing a decade
The socioeconomic circumstances of class
The psychological games played around it
The cutting misery of its unrequited wishes
All the words and worries and tactics it whittled into its block
Everything that everyone said and did to try to dull and deflect it
All of the arrogant antagonizations condescended as if absolute

The knife cut straight through them as it would warm butter,
revealing what's claimed to matter more than it to be
immaterial illusions; preventative preconceptions proven pretend

It made mincemeat of everything said to oppose
its will, dicing them up as if they were barely there

This knife that just as readily passed through my chest,
stuck and stayed, forever lodged in the one
sanctified place that captured and set it in stone

Flower in the Field

If you believe it to be you
You must fight to make it true

For, if you have a love for it, it's lord and master
To cast it out or kill it is to assuredly court disaster

For even if unrecognized by the
remaining whole of humanity
If it enlivens your heart and stokes
the romanticism of your mind
It's of more divinely-sanctioned truth
than anything so stamped by authority

Its value is not to be found in its financial remuneration
But in the wealth accrued within the heart and impassioned intellect

Its successes aren't made of social
media likes and the hails of critics
But by whether or not it touches that
which their tributes can never touch

Its appeals aren't made to marketability,
profitability and public validation
But to the Gods of Truth and Beauty
in whose temples it makes its offerings

For it matters not if you've cultivated an
entire field of economic yield
If the one esteemed flower therein

perishes from uncultivated neglect

It matters not if the popular patrons
pass it by, entirely blind to its beauty
It matters if those gifted with beholding
eyes are born with eyes to see

So keep returning to the temple, holding the dreamer's torch up high
Pass through the forests of reality's renouncements, ever looking lost
Ascend the sanctified summit trail that the cowards cannot climb
The *only* path peaking at the point where the clouds of heaven part

Stirrings of Sanctification

Dissolution delivered through our electronic enslavement
Existing as extensions of excluding, compounding capital
Killing in contraptions annexing human automatons
Men made to mice upon the un-wondering wheel
Wonderous women left uncherished, unknown
Incompletions completing material modes and means
Longevity of life voided in un-vitalizing victimization
Thinning, fraying lengths gone of girthing greatness
Disconnecting, cracking crevices of burdensome boundary
Shallow graves of comfort burying beseeching poets
Ecstasies excised through the covetous quest for assets
Brotherhoods butchered by cowardly lionized leaders
Emptiness veiled by the vain finding of fleeting fortune
Indebted chasing dreams, dreamers torn at the seams
Aimless wanderings revealing all, led by laughingstocks
Chains fettering fools with aristocratic ambitions
Worries binding the broken, casts called bounties
Heaving with the heaviness of fulfilling molded functions
Toiling within mentalities tantamount to madness
Realism, the realization of brutally ravaged romance
Garish finery fanatically laced around false apostles
Sensuality of refinement slaughtered by sexual exploit
Showy games of confidence and cash concealing the lash
Spiritual champions choked by the captains of industry
Brilliance bankrupted by acceding to capitalist accounts
Waning of imploring heart willed by waxing of want
Catalysts of unity cast-out as heretics and heathens
Refining richness impoverished by emptying enrichment

Salvation in the signaling stirrings of sanctifying Spirit

Beaten Back to the Bay

Drawn into the hopeful, multicolor-strewn dawn
Scarlet streaked with amber, arrayed dispelling of dark
Portent of perpetual promise, the callings of the lark
Secret unfathomed riches do new days forever spawn

Ushered away from safety, hearth's comforting flame
Bravely does he bank into the stinging rising of the squall
Headlong into treasure or demise doth fortune-hunter fall
While a lack of good fortune the frightened forever blame

Nothing given nor granted, only killing cyclone can save
Only *through* the ravages and wreckage may risk prevail
Locked into the sheltered bay, cowards of pristine sail
Mast cracked, rigging ravaged, heroic spirit cannot cave

Recoiling cannons scratch his surface, cutlass cutting fights
Sun sinking back into Poseidon's den, the frosty, callous sea
Buck up and back the bulwarks, sea monstrous company
Foolish faithfulness, adventure succumbing to numbing nights

Leg swallowed by the squid, black patch over plucked eye
Chest heaving, souring sickness, beating him back to land
Let me recuperate else perish, life's lingering demand
Return to hearth and home, to eat, to rest, to refuse to die

Pretenders of Piety

Servants of Avarice, of Self-Righteousness and Ego

All waving banners of their antithesis, festooned
with the falsity of their particular pretense

Crosses of solid gold and gem of he who
took the most storied vow of poverty

Renouncing and refuting the fallen
angel whom they secretly serve

Lands devastated by the machinations
of the pretenders of progress
The effects of their extractions
regressing us towards extinction

Sellers of finery wrought upon the crushing wheel of misfortune
Their wares bore as beauty, masking the ugliness of their making
All worn atop the emptiness upon which it feigns its fullness

Pretenders of piety pridefully
flashing the symbols of mythical deities
Burnished upon blood-stained swords
cutting with conflicting conceptions

Fairytales told as if truer than the
truth of the heart to which they're deaf
Misdeeds advertised and lionized, their
acolytes of evil heralded as heroes

Divisions drawn as if empowering individuality,
designed by the conquerors of every obedient individual

Schools scorned by Wisdom, teaching of
fortunes found through enslavement of body
and mind, and the burying of the invaluable

Leaders led by false idols, by the iniquitous
cloaked in golden-hewn empty ethos

Obfuscation cast as revelation, the deepest, darkest hole
covered in a bright, gleaming white of entrapping invitation

Everywhere the agents of misdirection direct
towards despair, leading the slighted to slaughter

The few true shepherds mocked and ridiculed, their
saving signs and signals, their guidance of grace,
rebuked with pious pretense sold as sanctification

Seek-out and save these shepherds before they perish,
alone in the woods, away from the herds they seek to unsaddle!

The select, tortured, unseen, unheralded few who may
sheer the wolves in sheep's clothing, and redirect
the herd from the ever-looming precipice
towards which the predators steer all sheep,
their carnivorous colluders awaiting their impact below

The Trouble With the Heart

The trouble with the heart

is that it can fit the whole of existence inside it, yet the right ones
fill it completely, all by themselves, leaving room for no one else

is that it yearns to connect to everyone to whom it extends
its tendrils, yet, once it's conquered and claimed,
its absent ruler cuts all such cords

is that it makes every misery feel as light and fleeting as a feather
on the wind, yet keeps it bearer awake with the weight of the world

is that it renders all the pain worthwhile, yet is the very
rack upon which the most torturous binds are bound

is that it is tied to every other heart, dispelling all
semblance of separation, yet in its incompletion
ostracizes its bearer, thereby alienated from everyone

is that it cuts through all illusion, revealing the only thing
that's real, yet hounds with heaping horrors when
hollowed-out of that one thing

is that it casts an image of every form of fortune
into the mind, yet mangles that mind with the
promise of fortunes that it's unable to find

is that it reflects and refracts and sings in endless reverberation
of every form of beauty bouncing between its walls,

yet is easily caved by the ugliness that beauty conceals

is that its calls block-out its ability to hear the calls of others,
and that it aches with the echo of all the messages
it sends to the mind unheard by its thoughts

is that its enemy is the ego, yet the ego so enslaves
the mind that it tricks it into not heeding the
heart, ever rousing its rebellion against it

is that it bears the burdens of every form of breakage
bore by all to whom it connects, yet to bind these
breaks it must break itself in turn

is that, though it torments and tears its bearer asunder,
it is of its nature to grow over even the most wicked
of evils, in order that all of it may be known again

is that it is as intimate with the bottomlessness of barbarity
as it is with the heights of heaven, as familiar with
the clipping fall as with the winged flight

is that it is as wonton in its weakening as it is staunch
in its strengthening, as eliciting of envy and enmity
as it is resistant of those who offer them

is that it is as doting on deprivation as it is finding
of fulfillment, as forthcoming with the aches and
the breaks as it is with the bounty which unity makes

is that it is both the darkness consuming the light, and the
light expelling the dark, pounding with the paradoxes of
its endlessly magnificent and miserable mysteries

is that it still belongs to you, and though you don't want it, you cannot unclaim it, because it believes in nothing but its own captivity

Noctis of Narcissus

In the glorious light of the pallidly glowing moon of night,
the child of unparalleled beauty is born
Gifted with every advantage over her female
competition, by her image is every man made to swoon

Yet, of every outward beauty and sign of strength,
ugliness and debilitation are being brewed beneath
Unseen by the blinded men kowtowing before her,
or the women pitifully greening upon her passing

Man's riches effortlessly fall into her coffers,
for the world pays only for the visions that it can see
For more lovely is she than the Narcissus Flower
which bows to its likeness from the eroding riverbank

Stinking of the sickly-sweet scent of self-adoration,
its fleeting form reflects off of the river's surface
For inwardly does the devouring darkness descend,
yinning the yang of impending correcting rebalance

And blithely does the false, fooling idol of femininity
carry on counting the teeming treasures of her time
For the eyes of Noctis of Narcissus conquer with
a gaze, concealing an inward stare of blinding haze

Her emblazoned hair as red as the fire of all passion,
consuming all of the wisdom she knows not to seek
In self-glorification she sings in relentless renunciation
of any daring to dive into the depths of the river

Do you not see the endless throng groveling after me,
ye deluded seekers of all that's been found?!

Yet, upon paying the toll taken by time, her face is
wizened, and her beseeching heart is finally heard
Turning, the toadying throng disperses into the river,
splashing her with all the chilling truths of herself

Hear me, hear me!, she cries, upon the now
cruelly reflective riverbank where vanity dies
Upon deafly drowned ears her desperate calls fall,
for those looking for what to hear, hear nothing at all

And those coldly dismissed during her malice of
magnificence crawl up slow and sure from the depths

We hear your long-submerged pains, they say,
for you can finally see those pridefully driven away

They tell tales of nature's defining equilibrium, the
taking of the fortune of the famed, of fate untamed

Nothing stays the same, causes call effect, the very
waning of the waxed moon from which you came
You traded enrichments found by the few for fool's gold,
so that your rotting riches may look well upon you

Seeming of strength to those deceived by common-
most sight, your inwardly weakening pretense of might
Once bursting with the treasures reflecting the
brightness of day, spend now the stars of nighttime decay

Pearl to the Clam

For the wading, the want of muck
For you for need, for me for luck
For the listless, what do you feel?
For the feeling, to feel what is real
For the moments, motioned in vain
For the pleasure, pleasing the pain
For the rain, wanting the pour
For the wanting, wanting no more
For what you felt, bleeding the vein
For the sentiment, seeding the sane
For the gladness, gleaming in real
For the seemingly, mass appeal
For the apparent woe, wait and see
For the knowing, you knew it in me
For the wisdom, it wants of you still
For the ignorance, rind of the peel
For the pearl, forward the bill
For the shucking, discard the kill
For the fullness, each of us awaits
For the misery, with love it mates

See a way out, speak of it true
For what matters to anything matters to you

Rekindle the Core

Beseech of all sorrow, but known to the few
Beseech of the name not given to you

But willing of flame, reborn of the ash
But building of burden but sold for its cash

But calling for designation, called upon true
What willing of want, what cost to accrue

In wanting to say, knowing not what to do
To frequent the following, of folly imbue

Of what you are to me, it cannot be said
Of saying any of not, for filling of dread

When thought of you here, of love once more
Of decomposition not, rekindle the core

Have you any sense of what seemeth of you?
Of a power untamable, of the total renew

Parchment of Page

Hunger of weakness, hunger of shame
Hunger from once not knowing your name
Hunger of believing, of what ought to be true
Hunger of loving, of tragically loving you
Hunger of flesh, of feeble body and mind
Hunger of wanting not, of all that I find
Hunger of needing not to need, of all self-reliance
Hunger of sensing that all my acts are born of defiance
Hunger of seeking what they say is already found
Hunger of hearing the voice that makes not a sound
Hunger of sorrow, of what can never be repaired
Hunger of crooked parallels that can't be compared
Hunger of falling right back into my body and mind
Hunger of never knowing the like of your like kind

And in feeling of flesh, the hot embers of need
Forever unreachable, the folly of deed
For what cannot be known is no friend of mine
Forever lost in hunger whilst I endlessly dine
I must know all that I'm able, the lesson of the fable
For what is known not, the bloody feast on the table
Consuming raw breast and thigh, carcass torn in two
For as you gorge upon it, so does it gorge upon you

And lest you sense some duplicity, let me say to your face
What you gobble with relish was bequeathed in disgrace

So knoweth that whatever I may seek, I'm likely to find
For what is kindled in the body is burned in the mind

Thus, may you know of everything that I wanted before
Before knowing the means by which to want it no more
This, the very prism through which all truth may be told
By which the barest of minds are made fruitfully bold
Refracting what you thought you knew until known untrue
Words whispered of how, when and why death shall renew

So keep twisting and turning with the times of the age
Keep bending and folding with the parchment of page

Of Life Ideal

Upon poet's pen alights the paramour,
all its endless aspect and form
All passion and purity rounding him
with every reason for philosophy

To cultivate his garden
as one with his heart
Sowing seeds simultaneous
of Spirit and soil
To be led by literary giants,
straining to keep pace
Bouncing between their
proudly ponderous footprints
To follow the finest form of
himself forever sought
Roaming from salt-spraying
sea to enshrouding forest

Ice-encased mountains and
cascading rivers curing unrest
Sightings of flight, tracing
untamable wilds left un-hunted
Burgundy-stained bottomless
flask of Zin, Syrah, Pinot
Black coffee over salty, sweet,
spicy culinary creation
Beethoven battling Back in
the sumptuous background
European cafes, crossroads

bazaars, Buddhist Temples

Prosecco upon promenades,
traipsing across Italian marble
Overgrown trails and rushing
river's catwalk of cattails
Steps climbing canyons saddled
with ferns and evergreens
As far from corporate incursions
as it's possible to be
Sweet silences beside birds and
wind-whispering, towering trees
Needing nothing but ingenuity,
courage and the stewardship of land

Artistically surrounded, struck strings,
keys calling soaring sentiment
Fare plucked straight from bush,
tree and vined-trellised gardens
Naturally-nurturing goats and
chickens giving back all they get
Discourse of all idea and principle
pursued with Ancient Athenian gusto
Blossoming trees of cherry, plumb
and apple competing for favor
Native medicines manufactured
from bark and root, leaf and flower

Women of leveling look, disarming nature,
commanding sensuousness
Knowing every shapely nuance,
the finery of her every facet of form
Enrapt by best-burnished brush and
chisel, and pen upon page

By the violin and the piano's partnership,
old masters brought to life
By ideological competitions, idealism
conquering realism at every turn
Proving practicality impractical for
making of muses and arising romance

Films beaming inspiration, beseeching
a return to when movies were art
Lawrence of Arabia and Doctor Zhivago,
duration unnoticed dramatization
Smoking salmon upon fires framed
by artists, thinkers, counter-culturalists
Caught in melody and collective
consideration, unafraid of 'argument'
Ontology trading with artistry,
metaphysical with classical accompaniment
Gathered excess relieving empty bellies,
burdens of beleaguered minds

Communities blurring the line between
private and public, profit for people
Efficiencies of sharing, merited distributions
displacing the classist calls
Age-old oppression revealed in Spirit besting
religion, inclusion for exclusion
Democracy taking over its pretense, the
empowered tearing down its façade
Suffused with all manner of making,
rising with the daily tide of inspiration
Everything of heart felt, said and acted,
without the restrictions of the realist

Idealism as having the imagination's

courage, morality made into reality
People following their hearts into its
immersion with one another
Everyone forgetting the false, conquering
facts taught as if the only truths
Traditional binds broken upon the
revolutions of the minds of the many
Destructive calamity reformed into the
mutualistic modernization of man
Feeling the rising force of an
evolution of the species honing heroic heart

Unconquerable Power

Oh what a fire burns within me!
That pushes my pen into poetry

That seeks the refinement of all that I sense
That needs only the moment's recompense

That probingly peers into nature's endless hues
That is powered by the love embodied by muse

That assures the pains of the past aren't rendered in vain
That blurs the line between rapture and going insane

That sees of life what it ever ought to be
That knows that only in love may we ever be free

That fights for the magic made all around
That seeks of the throes of passion to always be bound

That trades what's accepted for what the idealist makes
That vows to shield the defenseless from what the emperor takes

That learns more from feeling than from the thoughts of the mind
That knows of the heart, that consciousness follows behind

That is led by the everlasting, in every fleeting hour
That envisions of impending unity an unconquerable power

Everlasting Invocations

Of what bursting agony and effulgence is this?
Of what anguish does the miring muse impart?
Of what immortal makings do you elicit?
Of what effortless command of my aching heart?

How is it that your love forever lingers?
Heeding not time nor distance between
How have you subsumed the eternal seed?
Keeping my fecund cultivations forever green

Of what divinity of nature are you imbued?
Of what litany of language do you endow?
From what species of sentiment were you born?
To your everlasting invocations must I bow

To what teeming waters do you lead me?
To what mystical lands of everlasting longing?
By what pain of separation do you surround?
To what endless need is your belonging?

Why do you bring me here each day?
What is it that you need for me to do?
Of what mountain am I steadily making?
From the mounting matter made of you

When shall you let go of me, my love?
Though it seems that it's I that tie to you
For how may our cords be so tightly bound?
By but each of the knot passing through

Disintegrating

My heart waxes and wanes not as nature's nuanced gradations
But as the turbulent caprice of stormy weather offering no shelter

As an uprising of a crimson moon, failing to pallidly persist
As a painter that lustily cuts and bursts upon his bloodied canvas
As the uncannily carving sculptor ultimately cracking his perfection
As a lover so insatiable, he comes to consume all that he loves
As one that burns the bridges behind every chasm that he crosses
As the loather of all self-righteous show, all pathetic sordid pretense
As the vessel that can never be filled, the over-turner of satisfaction

As intemperate as tidal waves tearing at his disintegrating seashore
As they pull him a piece at a time back out to the ever churning sea

Fallen

Entirely unmoved by the magnificence of the mighty
redwoods in the resplendent forest of giants
which they mar so mercilessly
the fallers feel nothing

They are as indifferent to their doings
as that of the cold cutting chain
of their mechanical saws screaming
their violent intent along the ridgeline
as they bite their way deep into the
fibrous red bark of the behemoths
wedging their way into the weakening
precipitating the towering collapse

From my perch of pathos atop the hill
I hear the steady screams below
as the rulers of this country unwillingly
abdicate their ferny-floored thrones
peeling from their proud posts, pounding
the ground with echoing anger
their voluminous crash calling-out
the dishonor of the killing of kings

Crashes rebound all the distressed day,
resounding with a lack of regret
with the sheer indecency demonstrated
by the cold calculations of killers

One laughs maniacally as he mars, cheap

six-pack awaiting in his truck bed

The forest belongs to man, who, though
being but another passer-through
passes with such entitlement that his wake
may mark the end of all passage
so cold are his cuts, so inconsiderately
unsustainable his extractions

And yet the fallen forest feels no indignation,
and expresses no lamentation
quietly battling back, the macroorganism
rallies heaping hordes of micro forces
synergizing the rekindling, seeking the best
suitability for their reorganized roles

While we that buy the wood that builds our
homes await the outcome, as if bystanders

Spirit's Inquisition of Religion

You are not merely your corporeal structure
making matter of energy
You are not only that which forms for
the function of physical life
Not only the limitations permitting the pressures
precipitating evil potential
Not but which is formed from the finite nature
of my material manifestation

You are my indivisible, endless energy itself,
beyond creation and destruction
The eternal interwoven with every dynamic
element of my everlasting endowment

It is of the heart to know this, to remind
the mind of what it wasn't there to know
And no myths, no matter how magnificent,
may monopolize the makings of magnificence
My force is beyond all containment of concept,
my infinity found in every finiteness of form

No one symbol may ever mark my fullness,
for no one flag flies from my radiant ramparts
I am woven into every flag, the ink penned
into every mark, the inspiration of all creation

What need of a symbol for that
from which all symbolization springs?
What mode of representation for that

which multiplicatively mocks mimicry?
What more egregious offense than to
shorten the endless table of brotherhood?
What people may be anything but abjectly
arrogant in claiming possession of me?
What more prideful impudence than to
proclaim and purvey any oneness of prophet?
To not see that any whom speak the truth
of me embody the prophet during such speech?

What more undermining of humankind than
to force exclusion upon the fully inclusive?
What haughtier nonsense than to heap
hierarchy upon the everlastingly perfectly level?

What more destructively delusional than to
pretend to restrict the naturally unrestricted?
What greater injustice than to remove all
self-responsibility propelling people's proaction?
What more insulting to the mind than to dismiss
reason, and to sully science as unfaithful?
What more unappreciative of language and idea
than to make absolutism of all metaphor?
What more disempowering of my divine manifestations
than to falsely divide them from my divinity?
What more enslaving of all my living elements than
to preach to them the lie of separation?
What more misleading than to mentally mar
humanity with the mindset of being inherently evil?
To not know that good and evil lives in every form,
the fulcrum its relative strength and weakness?
That human nature is always good of heart *and*
corruptible through mental and bodily limitation?

Will you not finally come to see that all of it is
relative, everything being relative to me?

That all theology, except that which applies to
all theology, is but a page in the Good Book?
That I am as the ink, the philosophers and poets
the pens, the everlasting the book's binding?

Don't get stuck on one page

Remove the bookmark, turn the page, ready
to read of my endlessly gifted inspirations
For it is of everyone to compose the Good Book,
you being but a unique form of composer
Given this precious montage of moments to
pen your perspective into my endless aspect

Presence

I need not your body
I need not your words
I need only your *presence*

It touches me without reaching
It sings to me without speaking
It fills my vessel without pouring
It wraps around me without moving
Warming me with the friction of our shared space

All of me is filled when you're here
There's no room for anyone, anything else
I seek nothing else, for the vacuum is sealed
There's nowhere left to enter, no entry point
No pores, no gaps, no spaces remain

Everything slows down, then stops

Here, with you, I sense no passage of time
The clocks have ceased from ticking

Timelessness is love itself
It is divinity itself
That which cannot subside
For it is the only truth
The only thing that's real
So that when you come to know it
You know reality for the first time
You know that it *is* what's real

And that all else is unreal

All else is but the shadow cast by truth

I've known all of this in my heart
And it cannot forget it
For it is the only thing that's in it
The only thing of substance
The reality to which all illusion clings

And all the minds, and all the logic, and all the laws
All that prevails within the universe of appearances
Condemn me for knowing and being unable to forget
And yet the one truth forever remains, perfectly defiant
The one reality, radiantly empowered by your presence
You could forget every detail of it
Yet still know it completely
For what is known is not form
What is remembered is beyond particulars
Forever are the echoes of its everlasting essence

It tells me all truth when you tell me *your* truth

And it cannot die
For even when it fades from the mind
It forever dwells within the source itself
Always in its complete, unconquerable form

A volcano lodged against my sternum
Erupting whenever you draw near

Cardiac Call

Of all that I've beheld before
of sights and sounds forever more
of tastes and smells beyond delight
of garish day careening with concealing night
of all the hopes that I've long dared to dream
of all the deceiving fears never what they seem
of all the adventures beckoning me abroad
of all the cold capitulations by sad, consenting nod
of all that fuels the fire of my unrelenting passion
of all that consumes me beyond my ability to ration
of all the useless dependencies I'm taught to need
of all the hollow gratifications I'm groomed to feed
of every aspect of myself that I thought that I knew
of endless gradient of color in all my perspectives' hue
of all the towering delusions compelling ascent
of all the exorbitant interest extracted on everything lent
of corporate piranhas preying upon my every weakness
of parasites sucking away while conditioning meekness
of all that I'm heartened and honor-bound to fight each day
of all that I'm ordered to think and violently shoved to say

of all of it and then some, I know but one thing for certain
there's nothing without not revealed by parting inner curtain
as all truth arises without force, else isn't revealed at all
echoing divine truth, the beating drum of the cardiac call

The Ascent

Walking the crisscrossing, rising and falling
paths of life, surrounded by my brethren
Our lines are as the diverse terrestrial
litanies littering the unlimited landscape
Every feature and form is found, then
traversed, else entrapping us travelers

Some labor to climb above the bog to
which others seem fatefully bound
Mired in the muck, a great many wallow
like pigs fattening for their slaughter
Some lash at the limping, while others hold
out hands to the suffering and the starving

Assistance is provided at a price by most,
for invaluable rewards by but a select few
Those in pain, fearing they suffer in vain, seek out
and entangle others to suffer alongside them
They walk near those fat with greed, dropping
crumbs to the lashed laborers pulling them along

Gluttonous, the overfed cackle and drool,
expending only the effort needed to dupe the indebted
They call themselves leaders, even as the gullibly
exploited in front of them pull their massive weight

Those few daring to call out: *The contagion of greed grows among you!*
are spurned, and soon cast out from the tethered, laboring crowd

Most of these estranged few eventually capitulate to the cooing calls,
begging readmission, while but a few successfully climb up and away

These few gradually come to see more than the mired mob may see,
for their perspective becomes as that of the falcon flying high above

Those in pain wish pain upon others, they cry whilst
mounting the foothills, *for no one wishes to walk alone!*

Their calls echo down and bounce about the masses,
most dismissing them as the sounds of the fanatical,
the unrealistic fantasies of the foolish

*Those consumed by greed consume all that surrounds them, including all
whom are tricked to take heed of their greed!,* the climbing call continues

Listen not!, the fat, false leaders cry, *for I hereby
declare that you are free to become as fat as me!*

*Those that do wrong to others, trapping them in the lowlands,
always force upon others the wrongs set within themselves!*

Such calls continue to fall from above, rebounding off the sides
of the narrowing canyon in which the teeming crowd is caught

Listen not!, the false leaders flail and cry, *for those are but
the whispers of the wind, as insubstantial as dreams and ideals!*

*Those that enslave do so to preserve their own enslavement
to the God of Greed and Ego!,* the upper echo resounds
*They but conserve the carts constructed by their forebears,
whom your own forebears backbreakingly pulled*

all the way to their own unhappy graves!

Listen not!, the ever fatter, false leaders cry, *for they are
the naïve that see not your evil nature as I do, born into
sin and the one reality of the weak and the strong!
They delude themselves into believing in fantasy realms made
of unnatural, communist equalities that can never come to be!*

*Evil is but giving into the corruptibility born of mental,
moral and bodily weakness, so as to keep others weak, divided
and dependent!*, one cries from the mountaintop far above

*Good is but to follow your innermost strength, to fight
corruptibility, to help the many find and fight for the
best of everyone! Break your binds, brothers and sisters!
Let the misery-mongers pull their own weight!*

The shout is bellowed as if coming from the mountain
itself, thunderously shaking the stirring masses

CLIMB, I SAY, CLIMB!

Ablaze

You know exactly how I feel about you,
without my saying another word
Because the feeling is always the same,
even as its catalysts are limitless
It's the magic, the force of creation,
the foundation upon which all is built
It's the lost and found within us all,
the one original forever reinvented
It's as old as time itself, and visited
upon every space of existence

And yet it visits each of us, every
time, as if it's perfectly new
As if we're finding something
that's never been found before
Made unique through every
manner in which we're made unique
Forever recycling the kindling,
rekindling the fiery purpose of life
The burning bounty of being
brought up from the Big Self within
The gifts gifted to each self tugging
on their intertwining with the Self
The perpetually rewinding reminiscence
of Self's incarnation of selves
Witchcraft, the casted spells of
Spirit, the incantation of inseparability

That's what I tap into when you

open myself up to Myself
Just thinking of you, of what you
made me feel, the echoes of eternity
What else is there without that
upon which everything is built?!
Only towering edifices absent
foundations, awaiting crumble and collapse

I harness The Force through you,
like a ray passing through a magnifying glass
Focusing the brilliant intensity of
my beaming heart, so to set myself ablaze

The (False) Truth Project

Speciously the words tumble from the lips
of the deceiver, the false servant of God
Cried out as if of divinely sanctioned
truth, yet torn from piety's pretense
Backed by grand edifice, richly-embroidered
robes flow below his slithering tongue
He that paints poison upon a kaleidoscope
of sweetly enticing colorful candies
Blowing a bubble around his adherents
which no evidence, no reason may pierce
His talons hidden to all but those
with eyes skeptically honed to see

Tentacles entrap the gullible mob meekly
bowing before his pretend power
Surrounding the weak and desperate
tragically unwitting of their dire detainment
Thinkers and theorists ten times his height
made to midgets in the eyes of his minions
Greater minds granting liberation denounced
and dishonored, their limitless value lost

Science and philosophy cast into martyrdom,
burned upon his disempowering pyre
Purporting to put to shame all whom would
lead them to the true paths of salvation
Shaming only himself by his manipulated
misdirection of the descending masses
Those hearing mistruth made to truth

in their overly eager, meagered minds
Thereby made meager for life, perpetually
bound to mirages of might and magnificence
They upon whom he feeds, enslaved by fear,
ignorance, ethos and the need to belong
Every weakness within them he tells them
is strength, calling their enslavement freedom

The demagogue draws feebleness from
his victims, bending them to his secret sin
Citing holy scripture, he scours the land for
those to draw down into his dooming den
Locked into unseen shackles, countless peers
pressure more into the enchained line
Complexities dumbed down and untruthfully
twisted so as to dupe the deceived
All that is good, and truly of God, marred
and murdered by him in heavenly name

And so the symbolic devil, derived from
Hades, plays the part of holy messenger
Weakening, chaining, shaming truth and
honor through the visages of virtue

Beware he who holds beyond reproach what's
haughtily hailed as 'The Good Book!'
For to be beyond reproach is to lack the
doubting seed from which all truth springs
Without which you're set to swallow lies
which doubt divides from the façade of divinity
Else to forever live under the thumb and
invisible lash of imperial offspring such as he

This I hear in heart and mind, echoing off of

this seedily-selling, self-stationed 'man of God!'
This fallacious phony of sickening sacrament
making man to remain on his knees!
Where be the words of holy shield protecting
the vulnerable from such shiny deceptions?!
Where be the ways and means by which the
susceptible might be spared from such a Satan?!

Forever Bound

Where of the Spirit dare not dwell
a secret that time shall never tell
For whereas space moves through all
descent within itself its only fall

In it, a vision of every evocative sight
the softest caress of the darkest night

The light that shines from up on high
that casts its glow across every sky

Delivering all truth without a thought
the soaring bird that can't be caught

The force of all feeling, constant renewal
its uncountable wealth beyond accrual

Denouncing damnation as foolhardy fable
making every mode of which we're able

Sparking the ardor enflaming adoration
kings and queens of hearts coronation

Leading not into temptation, body and mind
such weakness within it, ye shall not find

Beseeching we release the once besought
to find a future less frighteningly fraught

And when our most glorious hours are found
it whispers: *to each, to all, forever I'm bound*

Sailing In

In arrogance, creation assumed
Yet in prisms passage Spirit resumed
Perpetual shining of perfect white light
Conducted through our hearted insight

We be but vessels in voyages unending
Of every outward sail, a return for resending

A Land Without Honor

This is a land without honor
Where the princes of darkness murdered honor
Where they wield the cutthroat sword of profit
Plunging it into the champions of progress
Slicing through every form of populism
Entirely beholden to the plutocracy they call democracy

This is a land without honor
Where most are fully mired in debt
Where you have to enrich a landlord for the right to live
Where you become bankrupt if you get sick
Where what stands for food is a chronic poison
Where 'enriched' and 'wild caught' mean unnatural

This is a land without honor
Where the descendants of the princes of darkness reign
Having crossed the Atlantic on the pretense of adventure
Only to murder and steal the lands of the natives
Then dishonor their culture with casinos and alcoholism
Building their base of wealth on the broken backs of Africans

This is a land without honor
Where the word 'freedom' is narrowly interpreted
Where it means 'free to do what you want'
Never 'freedom from the trespasses of others'
Thus, those that have the means to do what they want trespass
Walking all over, crushing and oppressing those without

This is a land without honor

Where a total ass hat, narcissistic pig played president
Where 'leadership' means manipulation and demagoguery
Where prejudice and ignorance are the staples of politics
Where those that speak for the people go unheeded
Where any positive measure made is undone the next election

This is a land without honor

Where the philosopher kings are left uncrowned
Where their words might be found on Barnes & Noble bookshelves
Set upon the least-frequented shelves of the store
While anti-vaccination books without truth are sold to fools
Their victims walking in unmasked, forcing others to flee

This is a land without honor

Where non-critical-thinkers are raised to see socialism as evil
Where those whom would most benefit by it spit upon its potential
Where the philosopher that disavowed all wealth
That said 'give away all that you don't need, and them some'
Is represented by men with mansions and jewel-encrusted crosses

This is a land without honor

Where 'individualism' has been harnessed by propagandists
Where everything is about dividing lines and oppressive boundaries
Where private property means 'you're not welcome here'
Where anything of collective, common good is evil communism
Where most are mentally enchained without having a clue

This is a land without honor

Where the rich get richer by the same means the poor remain poor
Where an epidemic is an opportunity to make another billion
Where men driving Ferraris step over empty stomachs on sidewalks
Where, if you speak against any of it, the scammed scream 'get out!'

Where to be obedient to oppression has become akin to patriotism

This is a land without honor

Can you not see it?

Do you not care?

Too tired? Took weak? Too busy?

Or might we speak about the lack of honor?

And seed it in the grassroots, watering it with the will of our hearts?

Overgrowth

Lusciously coiling chestnut curls become my bounty
interlace with my over-tugged heartstrings
enwrapping me in dangling, entangling weave

Eyes keep coursing blue, lustily laced with mossy green
as rivers rushing through soppily verdant overgrowth
fertilizing dreamy desires dripping with impassioned promise

Laugh bounce between the burdens of my brimming brain
beguile my reason with whispered rumors of romance
lightening the laborious load of my ever heaving head

Fingertips trace every scintillated swatch of skin
giggling glee grown in every moment's magnification
as we paint from the palette of pleasure's every hue

Curves cast me into the cauldron of unquenchable craving
brewed with your beauty, mixing our love potion
as we drink of its magic, spellbinding sensation

Within which dwelling of my being do I presently dwell?
where the senses finely hone this heavenly habitat
welcoming us to wander the shared halls of our hearts

Oblivion

Sleep befall me
Welcome me into oblivion
Let me loose upon the labyrinthian night

To grapple with my imaginings unimpeded
To be saturated in subsuming sublimation
To become the past in pursuant present
To find the truths condensed in the cloud
To make my mind as the swirling mist
To creep up on my unconscious quests

To bind the broken burdens of time
To peer past every allegiance to pride
To go against the hour-glassed grain
To ascend downward while falling up
To walk the waves of beaches behind
To follow the footsteps strung out in front
To faithfully traverse the paradoxical path

Here, where linearity is ever misaligned
Where context conceives its own crusade
Where infringing law is lost to cathartic call
Where I suture the scars of seething psyche
Where I lust after love and frequent my fear
Where I decant dread and get drunk on desire

Starting

I'm starting to feel your absence
You resound within the cavernously-aching void
Your presence the painful pang of unmet pleasure

I'm starting to see your eyes when I close my own
Those radiantly emerald, knowing, playful eyes
An endless sea of portentous possibility

I'm starting to imagine you in my bed
Rolling around, laughing, playing, kissing
I can scarcely fathom the depths of that delight

I'm starting to feel more of you in me
That subsuming sensation of core coalescence
The incipient stage of this, our sacred spiritual fusion

Belonging

Love me tender
Love me true
For I love everything that comes from you

Love me lightly
Love me with lust
For only in my need for you do I trust

Touch me often
Touch without fear
For I fear only the lack of you drawing near

Be with me by night
Be with me by day
For by your side do I vow to stay

Lips upon lips
Hands within hands
For it's all of you that all of me demands

So got not far
Tarry away not long
For to your heart does my heart belong

Every Flowering Field

I see everything that I need to see in your eyes

I see all sentiment snowballed into one brilliant cobalt blue
I see that snowball crushing, then melting my heart
I see that melt watering the seed of our relationship
I see that seed sprouting, fertilized by our fun
I see it growing by every energizing, sunning second
I see it blossoming, buzzing with bountiful life
I see us passing the nectar back and forth between us
I see the sweetest of hives being happily honeyed
I see us storing enough to see us through any winter
Enough to feed our frequenting of every flowering field

I see everything that I need to see in your eyes

Pastel Skyline

Pastels paint the Central Oregon skyline
The high desert is awash with its ethereal glow
It wraps around the linings of the low-lying clouds
Hanging so near to the butte-top you can almost touch them
Making of my reality as an impressionist painting

Bounding Back

There's no greatest strength without greatest weakness

No most empowering force of teeming heart
without it forever being about to burst
No greatest future not fueled by this
over-pressured, fissuring, fracturing force
No motivation to ascend the peaks of personage
without weakened knees bound to buckle
No knight of most chivalrous, uncompromising
honor without you, the meekening muse
No heights of elation without sitting here
holding you inside, feeling I may split apart

For to find my fullest life and best self is to pay
with the possibility of you grinding me to dust

So I think of you, I ache beyond ache, I pain
beyond measure waiting to see you again

I cast endless yearning at the infinite horizon
for the chance of your wave bounding back

All the Time

Sometimes I think that I just can't take anymore
Sometimes I fear the malignancy might make it to my core

Sometimes my heart aches without apparent cause
Sometimes the beast refuses to retract his claws

Sometimes I grow weary of wearing the weight of the world
Sometimes, before it disintegrates, the dying leaf is curled

Sometimes, around my heart, I can't build a high enough fence
Sometimes I think I may die without your love's defense

Sometimes I feel like I'm just too tired to take another step
Sometimes I don't know how past all my defenses you crept

Sometimes I don't know if I'll ultimately succumb or overcome
All the time, all I need, is for your eyes to strike me dumb

Need

I'm having trouble being apart from you
Even the second day feels like too much
I drink my coffee and try to read, in vain

My heart is too active

I think that it's calling out for you
I think that it's trying to cross the threshold
I think that it's attempting to conquer spacetime
I think that it's summoning spiritual gravity
So as to pull you as close as soon as possible

Maybe yours is calling out for mine as well
Maybe our hearts are building the unseen bridge together
Maybe we whisper to one another across the Elysium Fields
Maybe our tethered yearnings are defying dimension

Maybe *this* is what love is:

A reaching out with pure energetic tendrils
Tendrils that tie together, unnoticed by those around us
That pull you to me and me to you
That define 'God' and 'Love' by borrowing
the endlessness binding both
That usher the everlasting to pay
homage to this one aching moment

The moment where I can finally admit:

I need you

Oculus

Pinpoint plunge
Emerald-swirling ascension

Flashing focus
Dreamy disorientation

Naughtily knowing
Innocent enchantment

Wildly wonderous
Waxing wistfulness

Towering togetherness
Descendent departure

Seized by the ancient oculus
When your eyes capture mine

Crumbling Passageways

It is of the muse to be the bloodletter of good men

to know no bounds but the binding
to bewitch, bewilder and beguile
to bind the spell-cast heart to her whim
to make meek of those once thinking themselves mighty
to shatter steel ego like a pane of gaudily-colored glass
to stuff the will of the lion into the cage of the housecat
to twist and turn his guts, then tear them out
to expose viscera and make mockery of his pride
to vanquish vanity as the misbelief of the boy
to denounce all attempts to pacify and stake any claim
to make the birth of a relationship an infant strangled in its crib

to methodically take him apart, piece by gory piece
sliced to shreds, bit by bit, by her hidden dagger

to trick him into believing his self-consumption is filling
to find that he but reduces himself bite by deceived bite
that his insides have been torn free, turned to her offal
his openly aching chamber more expansively echoing than ever
He calls out for her there
her name rebounds endlessly, hammering his eardrums

But she's nowhere to be found

the phantasm in the dream turned into yet another nightmare
the pounding footsteps in his endlessly crumbling passageways

Harbingers

I pang with your presence long after your departure

It falls headlong and lingers, dwells deep, swirls, rises and falls

It disperses and condenses, calling creation in from destruction

It frequents each of my feelings, sharpening them into focus

It tortures as easily as it titillates, taxes whilst paying tribute

It pours as from a bottomless decanter of dreamy intoxication

It caters to every current in which
I'm caught and cast forward
As every river running every
ravine of reverie for the sea of sentiment

It reveals all that I'm afraid to see, every paramount portent

It seethes and spills over, refills and renews

It whispers of everything for which I've always ached
Whilst the demons decry over that whisper: *It shall never be!*

It's all hope feared in vain, the cost of all pleasure in redoubled pain

It surrounds me casting spells,
tempering beasts and goading the gods

It's the everything and the nothing all at once

It's the very reason for being,
the rewards dangled before my burdens

It's in front of me now, bowing with
a dagger concealed in its corset
Brought here holding hands with
the harbingers of both Heaven and Hell

Event Horizon

The black hole vacuum of being

Sucks in any potential of love

Passing over its event horizon

Hearth and Home

You need never feel the chill of loneliness so long as I'm around

For I want nothing more than to
be the hearth that casts away your cold

That burns away all of your fear,
becoming your impenetrable protector

I want... want... you make me understand what it is to *want*

I want to suffuse you with the endlessly-
emboldening blaze that you've effortlessly lit

To be your constant comfort, enfolding you
in the warmth of this conflagration that you fuel

To be your home, your fortress, your
safety set to securely surround you

To absorb you in touch and taste,
silencing all sense of separation

To make love to you as if our nights
shall know nothing of the dawn

To define tenderness in the tracing of your
lines, as if all clocks have tired of ticking

To please you as Adonis finally given over
to be gorged upon by the goddess Aphrodite

For when you're with me, so shall you be,
entirely free to be as your heart wishes you to be

That most sacred of celestial beings
born to be behind my shield of chivalry

To be honored and worshipped as the
sun that permeates every possibility of life

To personify the point, the purpose, the
purity pulled from the modern-day pestilence

To be the shrine in which I worship the
infinitely-formed femininity as if there's but one

For divine is your company, your
contours, the elation that you elicit

The everlasting force of all feeling
gifted in each of our overlapping longings

And so long as you set yourself beside
my hearth, forever warm shall you be

Rosebud

The bush is bare
Though I round about
In fear and frustration
I curse and shout

Desperately buds sought in vain
Watering beyond drenching rain
Fertilization far past every need
Foolish ever more killing creed

By legend, by lore, a bud doth show
Gripping, crushing, before it can grow
Overly needing of the absent flower
Prettily alluring, myself I devour

Lamenting, luring, honeyless hive
Deeply dejected neglected deprive
What weather, whether bud or not?
By what forsaken psyche am I caught?

For even when the myth comes true
I kill the love before its sweet renew
Hands and arms ever pricked of prong
Why by every season reaping wrong?

Why doth every blossom curse me so?
What of this bush may naught but sow?
Why bind me to its roots, oh Lord?
If by but bloodied thorns I'm to be implored?

Wailing, wanting, hacking frustration
Curse thee, oh teaser of emancipation!
Pull thee out, burn thee upon the fire
Yet seedlings surround, germinating desire

Equal and Opposite

To every action, an equal and opposite reaction
The hot air of passion blown into contraction
For by the same law as the psyche's creation
Was the groundwork laid in physics formation

To push away is to pull her closer, the game ingrained
Try to box-in beauty, confirm it can't be contained
For to show need is to feed the psychological beast
To sharpen the fangs by which she shall feast

The hot invites the cold, the freeze from the fire
Hustle ever harder, in more self-defeat to mire
Ballooning in sentiment, bring the pin to the pop
Chasing after her, in futile exhaustion you'll drop

As you climb her tree, fewer branches of which to cling
If she's not pulling you up, it's the plummet you bring
Birds upon treetops beseech, warning of fall
Up and out upon lengthening limbs, *Peril!* they call

To have not is to have, seeming to have no concern
To care not else pretend so, to conquer or yearn
A way around this obstacle ye, the mature, have mapped?
Delusion!, outside her sanctum shall you always be trapped

Telescope

Love resounding, designation displaced
Every lovely wonder, singularity spaced

Each feels fatalistic, the only that's true
Tantamount to the moment's timeless renew

Focusing, peering, the absorbing succumb
Achingly-bursting, the heart never numb

Intermingling beauty, brains and delight
But one telescoped star in fathomless night

I plot it, track it, calculate its composition
Conflating it with the night's endless rendition

It twinkles, teases, then blinks its way out
I vilify the vacuum with my soundless shout

It sucks in all of my love, building up density
Its gravity balloons to a galactic immensity

Going supernova it explodes, blindingly bright
The blast invades my vision and steals my sight

But as its death fades, the twinkling returns
So foolishly myopic, love endlessly burns

Urges

Every time I'm next to you, I have the urge
to wrap my arm around your waist

Every time I can see you, I have the urge
to close all the distance between us

Every time I smell you, I have the urge
to drop my face into your neck and inhale

Every time you touch me, I have the urge
to grab and embrace you completely

Every time you smile at me, I have the urge
to pull you in and kiss you deeply

Every time you laugh with someone else,
I have the urge to scare them away

Every time you text me, I have the urge
to describe love with every word

Every day without you, I have the urge
to drive to you and show you why it's wrong

Every little lack of you, I have the urge
to demonstrate what completeness contains

Unshielded

Misled, passions misplaced
Misdeeds, pure intention defaced

Bequeathed the burden of love abused
To valiant heart, to every hope refused

To weary of withering without the sun
To rot the root before growth's begun

To see the saintliness of love in all beauty
To be but deceived by my chivalrous duty

To possess a sword so sharp it cuts through all
Only to forget the shield when the war drums call

To tarry, to tether, to be bound by all trouble
To fight for our oneness, yet all evil double

To be borne aloft by every hint of adoration
Only to stew in the stink of further decimation

Where is this going, to a bright, finally ethereal height?
Or to a fatal fall off a cliff in the darkness of night?

Am I to be made stronger by struggle, or struggle in vain?
Cometh the sweetest reward, or but more souring pain?

Full Frequency

Frequency-mirroring vibration
Heart-mind melding consolidation
Increasing intensity overlapping
Individuality conception entrapping

Wave-casting confluent amplification
Energetically-mounting multiplication
Typhoon of cresting, tied-together tide
Heaping humanity, confederates confide

Empowering harmonizing reverberation
Populists pushing plutocracy's abdication
We the demand of democracy's authentication
Un-purchasable representation, our vindication

The Explorer

Of to the flower to bud to bring
Of spark-plugs to the spreading Spring
Of birds sowing seeds of which to sing
Of lineage lent from sprouts of King

Of new generations windward swept
Of burgeoning life of branching leapt
Of promises broken, all promises kept
Of buried bounty beneath Winter slept

Of seasons lent but to lose the light
Of moonlight confusing obscuring night
Of star-strewing heavenly lovers delight
Of decanting dreams, tomorrow to fight

Of love likened to lust, nature's promiscuity
Of multiplication separation securing unity
Of innate adapting evolving continuity
Of springing spritely morphing ingenuity

Of mountains to scale beyond all fear
Of drawing dread away to pull life near
Of manifestation making magnificence clear
Of epiphanies of all things becoming dear

Of happiness heaped as sand upon shores
Of chasing every desire the heart implores
Of pushing through all thresholding doors
Of towering lording over leaf-fallen floors

Of rivers rushing to commingling sea
Of cascading cacophony's symphony
Of salmon jaw-leaps for new bears to be
Of fleeting subsuming of the present free

Of storms battering cliffs, echo resounding
Of thunderous warnings of static compounding
Of electrical coursings security confounding
Of lines seeming straight yet always rounding

Of adventurous ambitions but courage needs
Of cancelling from weakness the ego feeds
Of cutting binding cords that caution breeds
Of evoking inborn explorer's liberating deeds

Siren's Serenade

Sailing alone

No safe harbor

Serenaded by sirens

Rock-wrecked and reeling

Patching and bailing water

Perpetually doomed by my desire

I am Odysseus

Destined to drown in the deep

Never finding my way back to love

Until such time as Strength ties me to the mast

Playing Poker

The first rule of poker:

You'll never win the hand

By showing her your cards

The only way to win her love

Is to hold your cards close to your chest

Until you're certain you have the better hand

For in this game, less is more

The less love you show

The more love you win

On Composition

Why be it for me to compose?

On woeful folly and passion's throes
On truths I'm told that no one knows

On sleeping sunrises lost, left unseen
On ruminations of what it all might mean

On dejection overturning fleeting titillation
On spell-bindings before cruel emancipation

On feeling every mystery unlocked within
Only to shroud itself and disappear again

On all the rendezvous lost to consuming fear
On the taunting of love never far from near

On all the places that every seeker should go
On propagandist lines the brainwashed tow

On false paradigms that progress must shift
On all the oppressive weights that champions lift

On plutocracies paraded as if democracies
On buffoons tweeting presidential mockeries

On every inspired feeling that finds my head
On every alluring lady I long to bring to bed

Why, oh Spirit, am I compelled to put words to page?
What is this need to poetically beseech the sage?

Be it only that I find my pen filled with ink?
That without this inked release into hopelessness sink?

Why?

Why grant me such hearted immensity
Such grandiosity of loving propensity
Just to endorse it as my existential bane?

Why surround me with such provocation
Locking every angel to endless instigation
Only to deliver me to demons to drive me insane?

Why this myth of the softer sex
Those callously casting all my love into a hex
Whom with impunity torture me without refrain?

Why this obsessive mind tied to unruly heart
Instilling every devotion which emotion may impart
Only to have it forever fissure from unrelenting strain?

Why make of my love a device
That manufactures all endearment into vice
Producing only perpetual loss for me to gain?

Why hold out the promise of all pleasure
The makings of ecstasy beyond all measure
Only to wrap them in a fabric of impenetrable pain?

Why grant me the sense of a calling
Heaping all hope up for the highest falling
Demanding all pursuit of progress be made in vain?

Why seed in me in every Christian sin

And the pagan origins from which their ideas begin
For works which only philosopher-poets can contain?

Protean

In love oft longed, shapeless fill
Any fitting form, change at will

In any color, empty canvas paint
Draw anything upon it without restraint

Most anyone may be made a match
All passing beauty it tries to catch

A most powerful vacuum, sucking in
Making into the thickest even the thin

You're the one and only, for you're here
Pulling you in simply because you're near

As Proteus, my longing may take any shape
I try to close the entrance, it remains agape

For solitude sickens when known too long
Clutching at everyone in the passing throng

Come one, come all, be not afraid
Overeager, unsuccessfully swayed

To receive what you want, want without need
Else be the festering wound, forever to bleed

Yet, how to impede in the need of this naught?
How not to care when so carefully caught?

To have it in hand, you must first let it go
Yet unreturning, but more loneliness know

Forking Trail

I was once of the walking dead

Of my ilk and I were the lifeless bred
Upon hopeless nothings was I fed
Upon nightly nightmares filled with dread
Upon listless mornings bound to bed
Upon countless opportunities which I fled
Upon pounding torments of my heavy head
Upon endless longings for which I pled
Upon mirroring melancholies which I read
Upon rueful regrets of what should've been said
Upon all sorrowful sentiment which I spread
Upon treacherously thin ice did I once tread

Then, clouds parting, a sun ray struck
And I pulled myself from the sticking muck

A miraculous uncovering of a fork in the trail
A wooded shelter from all which may assail
A flowery forgetting of every fear to fail
A natural shield against unsteadying gale
A litany of forest nymphs of whom to hail
A mounting multitude of brethren to avail
A mountainous ascension I'm proud to scale
A slew of hidden strengths to tie to my tale
A bracing of burden for those whom bewail
A force for fighting the evil I'm called to curtail
A certainty of the mission this trail did unveil

The divine whisper in the wind:

Ye shall prevail

Unlevel

Of the middle ground, of the easiest to do
Never a threat to me, never a threat to you

The level-most runways of the long lost races
The herd-tread cobblestones that time defaces
The transactional meets that memory erases
The commingling blend of everyone's faces
The summoning sameness of overrun places
Footsteps so overlapping they leave no traces

Here have I been accosted, lashed and hacked
Looking beyond, hounded, doggedly tracked

Go not to that place, condescend the masses
For but the foolish go where no one passes

Overgrown paths the few fight their way through
Ancient, buried wisdom in its unearthed renew
Where never forms the tired, everyday queue
Where, in hardship, the greatest character grew
And upon the cresting, grand perspective view
Riches wrought from doing what most won't do

Welcome to this place, declares the divine
Where in everlasting glory shall our sacrament shine

From Rice to White

Do you feel anything?

Does what you did have any presence?

Do you feel any of the pain that you passed?

Does any of the love that we shared, that you're afraid
to call love, that others saw and called love, all the
moments I remember so fondly through the pain, remain?

Is all of it washed away with the daily tide,
or do you ever swim in the ocean?

Do you ever dive beneath the turbulent, deceptive
surface of appearance, or are you too afraid?

Does the wave that we cast bounce back at all?

Are you here in the storm, or am I alone?

Are you here in my heart, or have you left?

Is there no longing, no regret, no reciprocation?

Is it all pride, all ego, all a shallow sense of victory?

Do you feel even the smallest fraction of this?

Do you care that you almost killed me?

Do you care that I'm now all panic,
all shortness of breath, all mistrust?

Do you care that I'm on the verge of heart failure?
That I've literally experienced chest pains because of this?

Do you care that I haven't properly rested since?
That my sleep is either too short, or too long,
and always interrupted by my psyche, waking me
to battle the monster hiding in the shadows of my room?

Does any of this matter to you?

Does it matter to you, or anyone else, that my mistakes were
based upon the weakness of neediness from more deprivation than
most ever know? Deprivation from chronic dis-ease, experienced
by one of the most passionate, loving, unloved people on the planet?

Does it matter that you killed a part of me, that I felt
it die, and that I don't think that it will ever be reborn?

Do you have any fear of what you've done to *yourself*?
Not up *here*, where you usually are, where you think you exist,
in this top-level façade of your being, but in your innermost
depths, where you know you've sacrificed what matters most?
Where your truest being knows that you've betrayed love?

No. You're at a party, and know nothing of such things.
But you will. *You will.* But no need to worry about that now.

Go back to getting drunk and high.

The Prophet Khalil

Every beginning is an end
A tearing of the tether we mustn't mend
Forever moving outward, the inward bend

That which I've felt, I cannot say
For words to feelings are as dark to day
Yet I need for you to know me, for this I pray

Only in separation have I despaired
Yet nothing known until departure dared
No contrast without incompletion compared

And approaching every love I know
As the mountain gathers the fallen snow
That from mounting beauty landslides grow

For none of ye shall see the heights
Without gravity's self-revealing flights
Only knowing the sun in the moonless nights

For there be no harvest free from rot
No free passage without risk of being caught
No truth is purely in pleasure successfully sought

Only in freedom from risk is there regret
Only the creatures of darkest seas flee no net
Only in safety of certainty are full lives left unmet

So of every future lover lent
Be they of every unknown torment sent
Every vision of direct ascension to be bent

And if struck by a shot from Cupid's bow
Pierced by a pain for every pleasure to know
From fertilizing blood shall your greatest self grow

And when love finally embraces you
Be of its sweet surround enhanced imbue
As the dawning mist blankets the leaves in dew

With joy, make of it a coronation
Yet demand of it not your emancipation
For breath too tightly bound brings suffocation

And from life, love makes itself renew
Every future from which manifestation grew
All journeys pulled from every passing through

And be it for charity to condemn the chaste
For promiscuously is all loneliness to be erased
Give of yourself freely, highest power embraced

And know none may own any earthly delight
To us, they're as the ships passing in the night
Lustrous leavings only when absent from our sight

And be there no giving with expected return
Ashen ego from the unquenchable fire's burn
Forever hollow, for all fullness shall they yearn

For to retain is not to gain

As deserted self absent one's own rain
Emptied coffers invite wealth without refrain

And being of a flesh to be sustained
Make not of other lives to be contained
Be they of the holiest sacrifice ordained

Eat of sickness, your sickness made
Mother Nature herself be thus betrayed
In self-plowed furrows, seeds of flourish laid

See of all the seasons in your reaping
In the soil of the Earth lies all life's keeping
Fall harvests growing even as we're sleeping

While to work is to fulfill your freest will
For the miller finds his purpose in the mill
In value-adding endeavor, no regret to kill

A love of anything to make of it more
A better existence, through toil implore
Reciprocal improvement, finding what you're for

Put it to production, else it's purposeless loot
Absent its application, all knowledge made moot
All passion wasted without the means for its pursuit

For, to put your heart into everything you do
Is for your every making to bind the sacrament to
By blood and brow shall your worth sweat through

And know that the more sorrow that you feel
The more ecstasy that you're bound to conceal
The deepest dry wells, the fullest wellsprings reveal

Your pleasure always masquerades as your pain
Always two sides of one coin for everyone's gain
Every piper paid, no evocative song sung in vain

And be wary of your own secure entrapping
Let it not become your preventative wrapping
Unwrapped presents, lost lands made for mapping

For fear, your natural home forsaken
Anxieties over your certainties to be taken
Waterfalls and forest dreams, never to awaken

Accruing mechanisms made to rust
Stockpiling amassments gathering dust
Walling-in walls closing in, flee ye must

For you're the owner of all that owns you
How your debilitating dependencies doth accrue
Surrounding yourself with what to fight your way through

Shield your ears from the contemporary din
For the untamable want beckons the wolf within
Hearing the call of the wild not, an unnatural sin

And know that every sword calls for its shield
As all hidden wound needs treatment to be healed
So shall everything concealed someday be revealed

And make the marketplace to serve the man
Rather than to take from him all that you can
Or by soft enslavement, bind him to greedy plan

And be of the conscience to treat transgression

And of the purified self to demand its repression
As crimes against others bring your own oppression

And yet, be merciful to the convicted
For in every image of evil is all man depicted
Of pain, hunger, desperation, none restricted

So study the spurring of the wrong
As the conductor seeks the balancing song
Punish weakness not, but make of it strong

And know that every law is relatively made
Just as callings are heard only by those bade
As every sun-warming tree casts cooling shade

For all too often does piety's pretense offend
And by honor the vilified lawbreaker commend
For he who writes the law, to his aims do we bend

And be not so certain your freedom makes you tall
For many an unguided ascension leads to the fall
As being entirely free to act is to be subject to all

First, free yourself from your own weakness
For from weakening action is born the bleakness
While oft is enlightened listening judged as meekness

For there be no yin without pairing yang
No melancholy tune of which love never sang
No defense against the beast without fearing fang

And delve into the heart's discord with mind
For only in their accord shall any peace ye find
Caught up in their war, by the ego to be confined

Agreement finds humility, hostility seeks pride
Purpose rides passion, reason's ruddered guide
Never be it for the surfer to make the waves he'll ride

And from your suffering you evoke the sage
For of the brightest love is born the darkest rage
And from the most trying times do we come of age

And make not of yourself something to be defined
For every vision of truth is to be variably refined
As you are your past, present and future combined

While that of what you essentially are
May never from you be but near nor far
As inseparable as the nucleus from the burning star

And when the star burns out or explodes
The makings of every function of form it unloads
Paving the overlap of every connecting crossroads

And there be no teaching born purely without
Only revelations of springs hidden in drought
A fertilizing of buried seeds sunning to sprout

Of ignorance only the self intercedes
Even the greatest guides be but your leads
To taste Sophia's fruits, *you* must water her seeds

And in friendship, know of reciprocation
Of symbiotic endowment in sharing creation
The grower doth grow from mutual cultivation

From utility may we ever find our way

And to use each for the other ye lovingly may
Only in the one-sided gain may love we betray

Love your friends by adding to their life
Of their burdensome binds be as the knife
Shelter them from their storms and steal their strife

And pay heed to your need to always speak
For from inner disquiet is this need of the weak
And the loss of complete thoughts you forget to seek

To refrain from speech grants great insight
So flee not from hushed spaces in lonely fright
The inner, unspoken truth sparks elucidating light

And know that of all speech a truth is told
A fear of coming across as meek in affect bold
Between the lines readings of wrapped-up to unfold

And beware the illusion of passing time
Which but the finite in you conceives as crime
You're both sand and hourglass, hollow and chime

The love of whom you most are is ever unbound
Forever beseeching you without making a sound
Forever revealing the straight as coming around

And know that from deprivation does evil descend
From festering wounds many care not to mend
From fissures and fractures of unmitigated bend

And when all of you is in self-accord
When body and mind are heart-implored
Then of every goodness granted can you afford

For, of much evil is goodness made
Of biggest lessons small judgments forbade
Of subsuming transgressions which finally fade

For of the ego, of greed infused
Of hopeful folly that becomes abused
Of every such vileness has virtue used

And call not upon Spirit only for assistance
But in gratitude for its inseparability's insistence
For between you and the One there is no distance

Extend yourself outward with every feeling
Get off your knees, it needs not your kneeling
Commune with the essence of shared Self-revealing

And here know the great joyful confounding
Of the hearing of Spirit in the mindfully sounding
Oft dismissed as dreaming what's actually grounding

And please, think upon the relativity of pleasure
For the foolish but hoard it as an accounted treasure
Dividing themselves from that pleasure beyond measure

For pleasure is both burden and boon
And may conceal the sun as the eclipsing moon
Like a double-edged sword cutting away too soon

So let your pleasures be tied to your growing
Let books be read because you crave the knowing
Let flashing lights be not simply show, but showing

And be of beauty to be born in reflection

For it be the revelation of every inner inspection
And she whom gives over to one is another's dejection

A weary traveler sees the dwelling as haven
Yet of its concealed traumas are made the craven
An unkindness abandoned but by a flock of raven

Yet seen with unassuming eyes
All concealment of beauty shall lose its guise
For even from scorched earth may more beauty arise

And be of religion to become all belief
To be of the sun-scathed, the cooling relief
To forgive generosity for having once played the thief

And make of it not a means to exclude
But a prism spreading all color for white to include
The looking glass through which our trust Self is viewed

See of Spirit all innocence and purity
The impenetrable fortress of entrenched security
The endlessly-revelatory antithesis of every obscurity

And of death, fear not an end
But a boulder around which the river must bend
A golden currency for the everlasting renewal to lend

In your heart you know all ends are illusions
That around it hover all of our fears and delusions
All flying away, leaving but the naught of conclusions

For of this journey, I must say goodbye
For it is not for the seeker to in one place lie
But for all places to be as brief amnesias in asking why

Fear not of my passing, for all truth returns
The out folds into the in for which everyone yearns
The inextinguishable flame from which the everlasting burns

Of the primordial seed everything grew
So seek not the finding, but the passing through
For what dwells in the timeless recesses dwells within you

Finally, let me say, certainty is darkness, doubt is day
For to fail to question is for the greater self to betray
No dungeon deeper than where you may comfortably stay

Post Script:
I Sat Beside Siddhartha on the Riverbank

A philosopher-poet and student of the great thinkers of the past, I felt that I understood much. Yet I was mired in misery, devastated by a recent betrayal. So I took a pilgrimage to the East, where many sages have found peace. There, my heart led me to the forest, where I met Vasudeva, the radiant one. He materialized from the shade of the swaying coconut trees, greeting me with a slight bow of his head.

"You are here to learn from my brother, Siddhartha," he said with a beaming smile.

I followed him through the forest to the banks of the river; the same river that had whispered the secrets of Brahman to the two ferrymen. There, Siddhartha sat beneath a mango tree, beside his raft, listening to the all-encompassing voice of the river, watching its endless faces reflect off of its surface.

Vasudeva blended back into the greenery behind me as I knelt beside his brother. My feet sinking into the mud, Siddhartha looked into my face, his own face full of serenity; free from worry, immersed in wonder.

I said nothing. He knew what I wanted. He knew by the trouble set upon my brow and the seeking locked in my eyes. He knew that I was in agony. He knew that I had lost all faith in life. So he began to speak, to tell me his tale, and as he spoke a soundless voice rose up within me like the mist gently rising from the river in front of us.

I took out my notebook and recorded what I heard...

I am here, but also not here, for 'here' is a spacetime restriction unknown to my truest Self; the Self dwelling at every point of spacetime.

Everything that pains me is of my small self, the self constricted by and bound to body, mind and ego. Through their needs, limitations and susceptibilities does suffering enter me; a suffering that implores me to divest of the small self, and to whittle myself down to the truest Self which cracks all whittles.

Only my body, and the ego and psyche residing within my mind, may fear any part of you; may fear your attacks and your judgments. For only they are frail. Yet they are not me, but the shadow of Self which you always inaccurately perceive. Always.

To fully trust in Spirit, in Self, to have the highest, unshakable faith, is to lose all fear, and to accept all suffering as a lesson offered by Spirit to all of its limitless ephemeral forms; a lesson that also teaches that, though you should employ those lessons as yourself, as infinite Self you are untouchable.

Say to those whom seem your enemies, but whom are secretly your allies, for all serve good in the end, even those acting in evil... say to them: Eliminate all of me which is untrue. In your treacheries, in your betrayals, in your attacks and judgments, my Self within can only become bigger; it becomes bigger by losing the false, unnecessary aspects of myself which you injure and reduce; my body, my ego, my psyche, and everything that I think that I own and control in this transient form of myself. I become truer, and larger, through the loss of anything which may be subject to treachery, betrayal, attack , judgment and reduction. What is true of me forever remains, revealed and enlarged by the degradation and destruction of what is false.

Patience is the virtue of needing nothing but the present. There is no void to be filled, no self to be sated, for the void is filled with awareness of Spirit, and self has been sated by Self.

We in the West have been bred with discontentment. For to be content is not to need all that which we've been made to believe will make us whole, and to know that wholeness can't be found without, only within; is to be able to go without all that used to control us for the covetousness of those sick with the insatiability of greed and the insecure ego.

You cannot be self-secure if you don't know Spirit. For Spirit is Self, and to know it not, to know Us not, is to permit but a false sense of self-security that, like the shadow, shall be cast in every possible direction of circumstance and self-regard, fated to forever shift and ultimately dissolve in the spiritual sun.

Fulfillment is not to purge, so as to forever become an empty receptacle, needing nothing, containing nothing. Rather, fulfillment is to wash away all that which stains and weakens, and to replace it with that which brings passion and purpose, and evokes the sense of spiritual inseparability which we call love.

There is no cycle to escape, no after everything that is and always will be, only an endlessness of infinite form formed from the forever formless One. To be inside the timelessness of the ever fleeting moment, to not be subject to the impositions of the small self, but to reside within the Self, within the moment, losing all subjugation to the needing body and the troubled mind and the misleading ego... this is the only true freedom, and rarely is it felt by most.

The less you have, the more you appreciate what you have. The greater the quantity of what you control and claim to own, the lower your quality, the greater your cost to life and the Earth that makes all of life possible.

The without matters not so much as the within, for the within traverses everything without, and when securely composed becomes less subject to what's without.

Those unsettled within seek settlement without, compensating for their intrinsically unsettled self with all that which may only ever temporarily distract them from their inner unsettlement, and for which they pay with the exacerbation and perpetuation of that unsettlement.

Of all knowledge, of all truth, words may only approximate what is felt. Truth is from the core, around which words swirl like a whirlwind, attempting to suck the seeker into their inner origin.

Thank Spirit that the transient form of self ends. You think people carry baggage? Can you imagine if every form of such small self sent its baggage on to Self, never to be unloaded, never to relieve itself, to relieve each of us, of the unnecessary and burdensome? Can you conceive of how heavy, unbearable and beleaguered such an existence would be?

What is perfection but the idea that something flawless may exist? And what is a flaw but the perception that something shouldn't exist, that it isn't right and isn't meant to be there, inconsiderate of how and why it was caused, what purpose it might serve, what it has to teach and what impact it may have had upon what, or whom, bears it? Perfection, one may find, is in the fullness of the fully absorbed moments; the moments when the mind is freed of flawed ideas like perfection; and in the discovery that what some consider imperfections are part of what makes something, or someone, perfect.

Nothing can be taught, yet everything can be learned. It is not for those called teachers to grant you knowledge or wisdom, but for them to guide you to the threshold which only you may cross, called epiphany; the aha! moment where you become more than you were the moment before. A countless multitude of people, places and things may lead you to the cool, quenching, replenishing waters, yet none of them may drink in your stead.

Fear not that you possess desire. Fear only that desire may possess you, and in so doing make you feel as though you aren't whole, and are deprived without it. Fear desire becoming dependency. The trick is to appreciate desire without becoming it; to want but not need it; to know that you're always whole whether or not you ever attain any of the endless litany of desires which you shall assuredly encounter.

One may be clever entirely absent the truth. One may turn words and phrases into the means by which the many, captured by the appearance of truth, may be persuaded to believe, to follow, and to proclaim obedience, even as they may thereby enslave themselves, and become proponents of their own exploitation and oppression. To see beneath the surface is the only way to save yourself from such a fate. This is the way of the doubter; the skeptic; the cynic; the artforms which many amongst the clever have convinced the insufficiently doubting masses are akin to pessimism, to doomsaying, but which are, in truth, akin to idealism; born of the will to protect those misled towards the binds and burdens of their own exploitation and oppression through saving ideas, principles and systems which the corrupt call naïve to keep the unquestioning in line.

It is not the overcoming of Self which spirituality teaches, but, to the extent which it's possible, freedom from self. It is the same as the search for God, or Spirit; the removal of the changeable, forever dynamically in flux fleeting forms from their essence and the eternal, irreducible force of creation from which everything and everyone springs. And when you find Self, freed from the limitations, weaknesses and false perceptions of self, so too will you find

Spirit, for essential Self is Spirit, and to know the one is to know the other. And here, too, may we know that Self may take infinite form, for it is without form, and must assume it by and through the evolution and laws of nature in order to make itself 'real' to the perceptions of spacetime and matter. Formless, timeless and energetic into the infinitely formed, temporal and material. Self into infinite selves.

Everything that may be perceived without may be found within, for there is nothing without which is not within. In fact, the separation between out and in is itself an illusion based upon the limitations of mind and matter, as both out and in are made and inseparable from the source of all things. Thus, when something is sought, quiet the mind and the senses and seek it not in a desperate search without, but in a silent search within.

We are as the water of the river, always returning, always changing form. From the snow-capped mountains to the ice locked within their crevices to the cascading falls, rushing rivers, resting lakes, surging seas and the clouds and rainfall and back, there is nothing we haven't been, and will not be again. For our evaporation, our condensation, our falling into the material realm and journey back are as timeless as the shifting of our forms, and constitute the very point of form: the inherent value of the journey.

Everything but the one thing that is all things matters only in and of itself. The one thing that is eternal is all things that are transient, including all form, and all the trouble and pain visited upon all those endless forms. Therefore, trouble yourself not, for there is no sensation or emotion without its opposite, and no 'good' not known relative to its 'bad,' and no trouble, no torment may forever remain. Relief and joy shall find you once more, in this form or another.

The best things, the greatest pleasures and fulfillments, cannot be taken, nor purchased, but must be earned.

Force nothing. The Way that you're meant to take is always open, you need only listen to the innermost Self pointing you towards it.

Weakness lives first and foremost in the susceptibilities of the body, then in the ignorance, ego and limitations of the mind. So long as these control you, you cannot truly, fully be free, with the degree of your servitude and freedom always being relative to the degree of such control. But begin with the body, for this is your foundation, and the more needing and dependent it is, the more it may crack, and the less stable and ascending may be the mind and life built atop it. And remember that, as you develop your discipline and strengthen your body, many cravings shall assail you; refuse them whenever you're able, knowing that by feeling and refusing to feed them, weakness is leaving your body.

The highest pleasure received is from pleasure given. All love is an act of reciprocation. For when it is not, it is not love, but the lust of greed in one form or another; a weakening addiction. If the conqueror isn't equally conquered, then his honor is conquered, and the higher form of himself is aggrieved and reduced until such time as he may redeem it.

Games of wealth, material, control, power, ego are as the chasing of shadows cast from what's real; cast from the love, energy and inspiration of creation which passes by unnoticed by those living lives in ignorance of the substance they know not to seek, and can never acknowledge that they lack, even as their truest Self beseeches them, its unspoken voice drowned out by the shouting of their shadow self.

If you don't follow the heart, heed its inspirations, pursue its dreams, you can't be your truest self, the highest self found when guided by Self, but have instead resolved merely to exist, to merely seek comfort and gratification, and to be as the ghost of the self unknown, and the life unlived.

The voice of the Spirit, the deepest, truest, universal Self, is as the trickle of The Holy Spring of Everlasting Life bubbling up from a deep underground wellspring of eternal love, seeping through the rocks, feeding and becoming one with the Earth; with the material plane and the endless forms which it hosts. To hear it, one must quiet body and mind, leaving only it, the foundation of The Holy Trinity. And some live such loud lives of sensory gratification and unsettled egos and restless thoughts that its sound is seldom heard; its spring seldom seeps up and through their closed minds and hardened hearts. Few bathe in this spring with any regularity. Those that do spend time steeping in this spring the Western World calls fools; fools for not chasing the ephemera of existence; for not being possessed by the false idea of 'owning' what can only ever be controlled and used; for not buying into the self-subjugation and popular oppression of the perception of power and the hollow gratifications of lust and gluttony and the hot inflationary pride of ego, the shadow self; all that which sickens those we've been conditioned to believe are 'successful.' There is only one way to cure this sickness: drink from The Holy Spring.

Most who are sick seek not a cure, but a concealment. For cures are difficult to find, and even more difficult to administer, whilst concealments are near limitless, making one forget for a time that he's sick through the very means by which that sickness is briefly buried, only to rise back up in exacerbated and perpetuated form.

The pilgrim has freed himself from his cage, from his trappings, from the controls of the exploiters and oppressors whom clad him and his brethren and forebears in invisible chains. He wanders the world, seeking, by the navigation of his heart, the fulfillment that belongs to inspiration, exploration, passion, adventure, love, and which may never be restricted or best belong to any time, place, person or people, but which is assuredly stifled by such restriction.

When one lives in the highest of truths, that one is inseparable from Spirit, from Self, and is therefore inseparable from everyone and everything, from the infinite forms of The One with whom he shares his essential identity, he understands that he loves everyone and everything already, and that beneath all trouble, all struggle, all discord and sense of separation there is only perfect unity and contentedness.

Beware the unsettled mind, for though it shall do you service to think, it may also do you disservice. As the rapids, as the falls, as the colliding currents shall it rush and roar in disquiet and discontentment, ever under duress, unable to be still; unable to settle and peacefully envelop you. But as the mean- dering river, as the lake, as the recycling sea shall contentment come, when its flow is slow and steady, cast forth without desperate urgency, or while chang- ing forms; whenever it's set closer to the certain Self that is always quenched, never distressed, riding easily and effortlessly across the planes of existence.

It is of the growing self to listen, the insecure self to speak; to show others that it has something to say, and that they should listen. When we compete for listeners, we feed our egos; when we're present, when we listen to others and the world, we feed mind and humility, adding something that wasn't there al- ready. This is why the greatest listeners are as the sages; they're always here, always growing, always becoming more than those speaking over one-another while hearing nothing. And of all that to which we may listen, nothing and no one has more to teach than nature herself, the purest manifestation of Spirit into matter, unfettered by the insecure ego and the unsettled, covetous mind.

Always changing, yet always the same. Infinite form, one former. Matter made of energy. Humankind made of Spirit. Mortality made of divinity. The seeming paradox of forever beginning and ending forms of that which had no beginning and cannot end. The very purpose of singularity expanding into an infinite plurality: an endless experience of existence by endless forms of and perspectives upon The One.

That which exists at every time and place at once, as all people, places and things, all forms and phenomena, knows only full and perfectly contented totality. To it there is no time, no space, no movement except movement through itself, no change but constantly deconstructing and constructing facets of itself. This is Spirit; God; the center of every being; the basis of being. The One Absolute Self. The only absolute, all else being relative to it, and only it.

White is holy because it is the absorption of all color; perfectly open, accepting and inclusive, like Spirit. For divinity is inclusion, the foundation of love, of connection, of the truest understanding, of everything good. The absence of color, the inability to see, the blackness of being and basis of all evil is the opposite: exclusion, division, hierarchy, disconnect; everything unnatural to the truth, and truest Self; the parasitism, exploitation and oppression that holds humankind in its infancy, awaiting its evolution.

Do not fear difficulty, for only through difficulty may the greatest fulfillment be found, and only in the certainty and ease of comfort do we dissipate. Thus, find comfort in the uncomfortable, see difficulty as challenge, and ever be wary of what comes too easily, for nothing of great worth may be thusly earned. And if it is not earned, then someone, or something, pays for it, or has it taken from them.

There is no teacher but experience. And though experience may take endless form, it is the body and the heart, the pleasure, and joy, and especially the pain and sorrow and suffering that are most instructive, for they stamp the lessons that they teach into the flesh, the heart, the psyche, making them indelible, and thus more real. So learn with the mind through the experiences absorbed by body and heart. And be not too hasty to hide from trouble, sorrow and suffering, for those whom reach the highest heights do so from missteps; from slipping, falling, paining, surviving and thereby learning how to step and climb rightly. The only mistake is being so afraid of falling that you refuse to climb, and, thus, may never know your heights; the heights of yourself and your experience of existence.

Flee not from your pain. Listen to it, dwell within it, learn to love it. For it is trying to teach you something. It aches because it has growing pains to bestow; because, from the fertile blackness, like the richest loam soil, there is a seed that has set out its taproot, and it wishes to spring from the blackness and reach for the light of joy, blossoming into fruition.

It has been said that intelligence is the ability to hold, and entertain, two seemingly contradictory thoughts in one's mind at once. So, too, is it for spiritual intelligence: to know that, nearer to the surface, in the realm of spacetime and matter, all whom we come into contact with are relatively separate in body and mind, in self, in relative form and consciousness, and, at the exact same time, are precisely the same Self as us beneath this, of the everlasting spiritual energy present in and composing all spacetime, matter, form and self at once. We are simultaneously ourselves and Our Self.

We all strive, all seek, always wanting, always needing, always pursuing those things which we believe shall fulfill us and make us more whole. In this perpetual discontent, this endless pursuit, is humankind mired, especially in the covetous, consumerist, classist Western World which stokes this endless flame for the sake of those consumed by the contagion of greed. Yet, there is only one way to catch this ever-evasive, fleeting contentment: stop chasing it. You shall arrive at your destination when you stop trying to reach it. Just as you shall catch your contentment when you stop chasing it, and let it come to you. If you are meant to be there, meant to attain it, there you already are, and attain it you already have.

Seek nothing, find everything. Let your lure drift in the calm, centered current of your mind, in the openness of your heart, and it shall catch everything you shall ever need.

One who is wholly open, who has stepped outside his ego, shall see that all people and all things are teachers, and that the greatest teachers are also the greatest students because they learn from everyone and everything, in their present, more than others. One who openly absorbs as much as possible, and freely passes what they absorb onto others, is always taking in while giving out. Be like them. Be not the corralling, controlling, hoarding dam, but the freely flowing river, everything coming into you, passing through you and continuing downstream towards all whom may benefit by it.

Reincarnation is not of a divided, individual 'soul,' but of an eternal recycling of shared essential Self of the purest indestructible source energy at the irreducible core of all things. That which I most truly am is the same as all things, always has been and always will be, had no beginning, has no end, and is both formless and all forms at once. Only the body and mind suffer for the sake of the pleasures and fulfillments of physical existence, and for the mortality of the individualized form that makes life so fleetingly sweet because it ends. But never forget that that is not who, or what, we truly, essentially are.

The more that you love something, the more that you know and appreciate it; its every nuance, its every imperfection that becomes perfect because it is a part of it; part of that which you've revealed your connection to more clearly than all else to which you're also connected, unrevealed. For all of these are actually the same thing: love, understanding, appreciation, perfection, connection. The closeness to the commonality shared by all things. The universally-shared spiritual identity. Self. For Self is love.

Pay less attention to the particular words, their order and structure and nitpicked meanings and translations, and more to the feelings and instinctive sense of wisdom which they evoke. Think of language like a guidepost: it can lead you to the truth, but is never the truth itself.

We climbed onto his raft, and as Siddhartha paddled me across the river, he ended the story of his journey and lessons with these words:

Beneath the tumultuous, restlessly waving surface of the waters reflecting the world of appearances, the world of competing forms, the world of endless change, of beauty and ugliness and the pleasures of the flesh, and suffering so severe it sometimes seems it'll end us, is a calm, endless depth of love that never changes and never goes away. It is that love that is the truth; that which always has been and always will be, regardless of the forms we take and the fights we make on the surface that seem so important, but which are all fated to fade with the shifting winds, floods, tides and currents of the seasons.

With a bow, I thanked Siddhartha for reminding me of The Way that I had lost. I returned to the West, feeling a sense of peace that I never before had. Since that pilgrimage, I pour over these words when I feel ill at ease; when I'm sickened by fear and worry. I remind myself of Our Self, and let go of myself enough to return to the riverbank.

ABOUT THE AUTHOR,
BY THE AUTHOR

Born in the redwoods of coastal Northern California in the blue collar town of Fort Bragg, my early years were trouble-free times of active, youthful exuberance. I was very much a rural kid, playing sports with friends, catching critters, exploring the forest, shooting bb guns, swimming in the river and ocean and eating blackberries off the bush until my hands were stained purplish-black and my stomach ached. At the age of six my father was transferred to the rapidly urbanizing town of Santa Rosa, CA, in the heart of the Sonoma County Wine Country, an hour north of San Francisco. There, I gradually transformed into a video gamer with a strong creative streak. In my adolescence I concocted elaborate games for friends that captured their attention for hours on end, often during school hours. Some of these games were centered around toys, but the more popular were produced on paper, which I called "paper games."

As I matured I came to the same conclusion that most young, observant people come to: money is the root of freedom, for freedom is *purchased*, not freely given. I knew that I had to do everything possible to accrue as much cash as possible, so that I could do what and be who I pleased. This culturally-pervasive mindset continued through most of college, during which I attended the University of California at Santa Barbara and studied Business Economics, entering the real estate business post-graduation. I was highly motivated by the orthodox ambitions inculcated into western youth by way of our aristocratically-hailing conservative culture and, through them, decidedly driven to pursue what most consider the hallmarks of 'success:' a lucrative career, the socioeconomic rank and all the trappings. This was before I realized the subjectivity of 'success,' and the fact that the greater form is that which Einstein alluded to: "Try not to become a person of success but, rather, try to become a person of *value.*"

Thus, I'd begun developing doubts during my last couple collegiate years that following the traditional path was what I was meant to do; that it was the best use of my abilities. Upon inspection, and in tracing the full causality, I realized that this path produces parasitism and suffering. The more you're said to 'make,' the more you *take.* Nothing materializes from nothing, and capitalism unbalanced by socialistic principles and equity sharing is less about freedom and hard work than exploiting disadvantage.

My heart and conscience thereby began to coalesce around the greater concept of success: defining it in terms of the *creation* rather than the *extraction* of value. Later, as my spiritual awareness grew and I began to sense that 'listening to your heart' is more than mere fleeting emotion, but a tapping into a truer, fuller form of universal Self, my earlier doubts began to crystalize along with my ideology and convictions, and everything changed for me. Though I continued to struggle with some serious health issues at the time, much of which continues to plague me, on another level I came into myself and began to harness a deep sense of purpose. I realized that I'm meant to translate the spiritual messages I receive which, combined with my intellectual inspection of the world, have led me to some profound conclusions about the nature of existence and the greedy heart of western culture compromising our collective potential. My innate creativity found a grander outlet in conjunction with my naturally-philosophical mindset, and I began seeking the underlying nature of reality, formulating my own ideologies and envisioning the type of societal systems that might someday steer humankind away from a 'greed is good' attitude that necessarily short-sells total quality of life on Earth.

As of 2022, my list of literary projects includes:

Infinite of One, All for One IS One for All
Heresies of a Heathen, Revelations of the Spiritual But Not Religious
Veritas Ex Spiritu, A Penned Pursuit of Spiritual Truth
Rosebud, A Poetry Collection
Love of Wisdom, Philosophy in Verse
Thin Line Between, Poetry of Illusory Divide
From the Roots Up, A Spiritual, Progressive Philosopher's Notebook
Avant Garde
Chloe in the Present
ANIMALS Party
The House on Apple Blossom Lane
Lucid (screenplay)

Access all of my books, papers and videos @ infiniteofone.com